WINTER'S COLD GIRLS

Dagger Editions (an imprint of Caitlin Press Inc.)
8100 Alderwood Road,
Halfmoon Bay, BC V0N 1Y1
www.daggereditions.com

Cover design by Vici Johnstone
Cover art by Sheryl McDougald
Text design by Sarah Corsie
Edited by Adèle Barclay
Printed in Canada

Caitlin Press Inc. acknowledges financial support from the Government of Can-
ada and the Canada Council for the Arts, and the Province of British Columbia
through the British Columbia Arts Council and the Book Publisher's Tax Credit.

Library and Archives Canada Cataloguing in Publication

Title: Winter's cold girls / Lisa Baird.
Names: Baird, Lisa, 1979- author.
Description: Poems.
Identifiers: Canadiana 20190119896 | ISBN 9781773860176 (softcover)
Classification: LCC PS8603.A44396 W56 2019 | DDC C811/.6—dc23

WINTER'S COLD GIRLS

poems by Lisa Baird

Dagger Editions

Table of Contents

I.

II.

III.

IV.

I

WINTER'S COLD GIRLS

All words transcribed from the Hawthorn Farms seed catalogue

They like winter's cold girls
frozen in rows—blanched
candy beauties. They are
not gentle with their collections.
They like them tight, inside
bottles.

Not this birdhouse
wildling,

    this veined twisting

       tiger,

          this giant

      bloody

        boil.

They wonder

Why these hot thorns?
Why these problem nights in red?

and

How did this one punch through the glass?

Welcome to the Museum of Artistic Apology

In the first room, a classic water colour
apology quartet: a series of self-portraits
of the penitent's mouth
shaping each of the four syllables
of *I'm so sorry.*

Next, a massive photograph of apology graffiti:
AMY, I'M SORRY ABOUT LAST NIGHT
stencilled across the Bank of Montreal's
west-facing wall.

Around the corner, a single
apology haiku found inside a stall
in the women's washroom
of a gay bar:

I didn't mean it
I really really miss you
Please do come home soon

At the textile exhibits
you can view apology hankies
embroidered with *I humbly beg your pardon*
along each edge, apology catnip mice
sewn for cats left out in the rain,
and at least one pair of sturdy woolen
apology socks knitted by a mother-in-law
who can't—or won't—speak about feelings,
but after seven years has decided
you're in the family to stay
and may as well have warm feet.

The Museum of Artistic Apology
is carefully curated.
There is no fauxpology art here,
no *I'm sorry that you feel that way* sculpture,
no song or dance about whether
offence was intended.

On the second floor, an entire kitchen suite
with carefully shellacked recreations
of the sincerest apology meals: made-from-a-mix
brownies, elaborate lasagnas & quiches—
many foods involving chocolate and cheese.

In a small nook nearby, photographs
of several apology tattoos,
briefly popular in the late nineties
and often involving animals: a weeping snake
curled around an ankle, a shoulder blade
framing a regretful falcon with
I hate that I doubted you
in cursive script below.

On the top floor, the rarest
of apology art, that of adults made
for children. Fourteen *I didn't mean
to shout* handmade dolls,
an *I'll Try Harder Next Tuesday*
teddy bear, a collaborative
*We are sorry that we're fighting
with each other but we will never
stop loving you* apology quilt,
and, spooling out over an entire corner,
a carefully painted wooden train set
with a hand-lettered note: *Even when I get mad,
you are still the conductor of my heart.*

Down the road, the Museum of Amnesty & Forgiveness
is a wide empty room—each wall a window,
the ceiling a skylight. It is unstaffed.
You decide if and when you enter,
how long you stay,
and whom you take with you.

FACTS ABOUT DEAD TREES
after Mindy Nettifee

Daddock is the word for the heart of a dead tree. When a tree rots from the inside out, it makes a long low moan audible only at night.

Dendrochronology gleans histories of air and wind from the growth of tree rings— proof that in order to learn about something you must kill it and cut it open.

The night my grandma had the stroke, I was a forty-minute helicopter ride away from anyone, in a forest which knew me in every mood, sitting in a firetower, a hundred feet off the ground while lightning stabbed its god fork, there and there and there.

The night my grandma had the stroke, my father called hoping to punch me with the news, to drag me by the hair across an unfinished wood floor.

After I hung up on him I saw six dry strikes and didn't call them in, ignored the blaring forestry radio, dared the storm to come closer. I watched puffs of smoke quickly quenched by advancing raincloud, watched the sky start fires and put them out like an eight-year-old playing with matches and a watering can.

Clearcut, a forest looks like shaved patches from above, the dog's abdomen after surgery. They did not invite me to the funeral. I am still pulling out splinters.

When the oldest trees topple, they give their bellies to sapling. I remember her looking out the window while folding pastry, her gentle hands, how she gave, and forgave.

The summer my grandma died, I flinched whenever the phone rang. Ran outside naked each time it rained.

HEX

Constipation so severe
you insert a spit-slick finger
to the third knuckle.
A shaky internet connection,
pinwheeling every time
you hit send or confirm.

To notice your only friend fears you.
To fall asleep again
with the TV on. Yesterday's snow
encased in ice at the end of the driveway.
To talk to the empty chair. To trace the shape
of redemption, too late.

Accusing eyes at family gatherings.
Dry rot in the walls.
A sparsely-attended funeral.
A grammatically flawed
epitaph.

GALAXY

I can't stop bleeding. Two
and a half months and my uterus
with so much to say:
clots uncurling, scarlet sea
creatures in the toilet bowl,
passed down slick and hot.

It's not good to hold grudges,
they solidify. Each unwanted
ass grab, cat-call or dry thrust
at seventeen, eighteen
nineteen, thirty-two—
lodged at the red centre of me.

I tantrum, twist, flail, gather purple
clover, sip cups of tea as if plants
could change the weather,
hoping to someday
call this catharsis,
as old flesh

tears free,
leaving galaxies
in every dark stain.

TAMPAX LOVES YOU, GIRL

w
a
s
h
y
o
u
r
h
a
n
d
s
before
bottle bleach
inserting
bare bulb
fluorescence
extension
of the
applicator
pray advil
assume the
position
pray contain
one leg on
the toilet
for seven days
aim at your back
none will smell
remember
relaxing makes
dead cells

trickling
much easier
from a musky
cleft

Athena Finds the Medusa Entry in the World Encyclopedia of Greek & Roman Mythology

After Poseidon, God of the Sea, raped Medusa in the temple of Athena, Athena punished Medusa by transforming her hair into a mass of writhing snakes. To look upon the horror of Medusa was to be turned instantly to stone. Years later, Athena lent her shield to the hero Perseus so that he could cut off the head of Medusa. Athena then wore Medusa's face on her shield.

No. I never blamed her. It haunts me
still—that slight form crumpled on the floor,
thighs bloodied. A god-sized hurt,
and the stench of seaweed

that lingered for weeks. If I'd come back
thirty minutes earlier. To spear him
like a fish on his trident. I did
what I could. Heated bathwater

each morning, made her eat
at least once a day. When
she finally spoke, it was to beg
for serpents. A venomous halo,

so if another man even looked at her—
I couldn't say no. I knew that history
would twist us. Even today, no one believes a woman
would choose power like that

over beauty. After she left I re-consecrated
that place to protection. Women and girls
came from all over the island
to learn to gouge at eyes

and kick at groins, to shatter collarbones.
To pray with muscle and knuckle. To shake
the temple roof shouting *NO NO NO*.
They don't mention that either.

Instead, they say her murder
was my fault. Each day, a swing
between numbness and choking
on this atlantic fury. So yes,

that's her face.
To remind me of the slow
gleam of the sun before
they buried it.

The Word for Secrets

The bleeding is supposed to stop once he goes on hormones, but it just gets worse. One doctor tells him *It's like estrogen and testosterone are fighting inside you.*

When a hurt person hurts you, how much of that story is your own?

He twists and spasms, he medicates far over the recommended dose, he soaks every towel in the house each month.

You tiptoe, duck, clean up.

What's the word for secrets that are supposed to keep you safe, but don't?

The gynecologist won't let you accompany him for the required pelvic exam. You sit in frayed silence, read the same page of a magazine. In seven weeks, your lease ends.

He has no idea that you're moving out once he's safely through surgery.

You have your second-last fake orgasm the morning before the surgery. The waitlist at the local hospital is months long so you borrow a friend's car and drive to a nearby town.

He tells you *I've never let someone care for me like this before.*

He wears his baseball cap into the operating room. They say he'll be out in three days. They keep him for five. The most hostile nurse looks like Leslie Feinberg in femme drag.

You find a small hostel nearby. Each night, you do not sleep on the floor by his bed. He is alive, and you are alone.

You exhale for the first time in over a year.

You pretend not to be afraid he'll die, while secretly wishing he would.

You give him a letter: *I love you, but I need us to live separately.* He screams, sobs and drools. You rock him like an infant. He accuses you of leaving him *in stages*.

What's the word for what queers leave unsaid so that straight people don't think we're irredeemably fucked?

The night he coughs and the stitches burst open, you've just smoked a joint. You stare at the carpet.

There goes the damage deposit.

How much longer does a bleeding person wait in emergency when they're a transman with a poorly healing abdominal incision?

The resident on duty is bored. It's late. You're charming as you slip into conversation *My friend's bleeding in the next room. Do you have a minute?*

The lease expires. You move out. A week later, you end it. He always said he'd kill himself if you left.

What's the word for the risk you take to save your own life?

Things That Evoke Intolerable Anxiety after I Leave Him, in Alphabetical Order

Basement apartments
Cardboard moving boxes from the liquor store
Chest binders
Dark-rimmed glasses & sideburns
Hospital waiting rooms
Police officers
Radiohead's *Pablo Honey* (1993), *The Bends* (1995) and *OK Computer* (1997)
Razors
Sex at night
Sex in the afternoon
Sex in the morning

Aftermath

She keeps spent light bulbs,
wraps them in tissue saved from birthday parties,
stows them in stacked boxes,
labeled as close as she can get
to the exact time the tungsten fragmented.
She holds a service for each one,
weeps over the first few dozen,
but there are hundreds now. She is old.
Next spring she will empty the closets,
unpack every row in the basement,
take shovel to earth along the lane
and bury each bulb,
grow dark flowers
from dead light.

II

BURNPILE

all words transcribed from the Hawthorn Farms seed catalogue

It wants to press
you flat. You can
feel it midribs—on bad
days, like a buffalo
standing on your
inhale.

Go back & empty
that house. Make
a heap in the yard.
Throw in the grinding
clocks with their blistered hours.
The papered-over insomnia.
The spineless cardboard
angels. All the years
you were easy
harvest.

Every brittle, wilted
heirloom. Even your name
is a catalogue
of overheated seeds
on the yellowing wind—
remember
what you came here for
& speak it like a bloom
of trumpets.

Do not ask
the fire to cleanse
anything. Just stand
close. Body steaming.
Eyes clear.

By the Train Tracks, Late December

Let's forget everything
we burn. Let's stand,
shoulders hunched against
the cold, a ragged ring around
a fire built of two-by-fours studded
with nails, coaxing it past smoulder
to blaze with journal pages,
high-school homework
and to-do lists.
Let's feed it all to the flames
on the darkest night of the year—
a hundred backyard bonfires,
a thousand quiet tantrums
hasty essays & faded blues,
combusting like tired stars.

Let's confuse forgetting with letting go,
drifting away later like moths
after lights-out, wondering
at the smell of smoke
on our coats, thumbing strange
keys in cold pockets.
Let's erase memory's bursting
cyst, mourn the backstory
like a punched-out tooth,
return to grope through cold
ash in morning, hoping for old fire
to scorch numb fingers.

To the Anti-Abortion Organization That Spent $91,000 to Build an Abortion-and-Miscarriage Grieving Garden with a Statue of Jesus Holding a Dead Baby

Do you
really
think

no one
has noticed

you
conjuring
guilt

&
calling it
grief?

Things Found in the Forest

That was the year Spring came on fast and hot
like the dog waking you by panting in your face.

You didn't even know you'd fallen asleep
on the couch, the blanket slid to the floor,

now you're ripping down to the river in bare feet.
The trees grown over where the dump used to be—

the several metres of overgrown, of lush,
of bugs and small quick creatures in the greenery,

of mud hugging the bank, this living, undulating strip—
Things found in the forest: catnip and nettle, broken

bottle, river turtle. Baltimore oriole, canada goose, dog shit,
a sodden pair of jogging pants draped over a branch.

Feminist graffiti on a bench: *HOES BEFORE BROS.*
Dandelion dandelion dandelion. A disintegrating shopping bag

from that yoga store: *Do one thing a day*. Here at the river bend,
the fast hot Spring shakes you out of yourself.

You weren't ready for the wider sky.

Reasons for Ambivalence about Growing My Hair Out

The direct relationship between the length of my hair and how often someone assumes I am married.

How awkward it can be when I correct them.

That long hair does not scream queer like an asymmetrical pixie cut.

That time in second grade, when Sean Atherton grabbed me by the hair and slammed my head against the blackboard, the classroom spinning around his blurred laughing mouth and a hot golf ball blocking my esophagus.

How I smiled back at him, sharing the joke.

That thing where the longer my hair gets, the more men try to take heavy boxes from me, hold doors for me, and approach me smiling with offers of help I don't need in hardware stores.

That I am not supposed to enjoy this but sometimes I do.

That the longer my hair gets, the better directions I get from strangers when I am lost.

The four-year-old who has me lie on the living room floor, brushes my hair out across the carpet, calls me a mermaid.

The winter I was sixteen when I hid my waist-length ponytail under a thick toque, wore baggy corduroys with a navy-blue wool coat that doubled my girth and reveled in passing as a short round dude every time I took the long way home from downtown Kingston.

The night I heard a woman shriek in Victoria Park and froze, needing to find her and too scared to move until another woman came by and we searched together, found no one.

How satisfying it was to shave my head when I left Kingston.

That the longer my hair gets, the more I look like my mother.

(Which would probably upset her if she ever looked at me.)

How hard it is to know what should be cut and what is for keeping.

Amy

He was the first boy to grow his hair long in seventh grade.
I'd watch him from across the schoolyard, smoking

and scowling, hands thrust deep into the pockets
of baggy corduroys. He was the only boy

I wanted, even after I asked him to dance
at eighth grade graduation and he responded *Sure, Amy*

—which wasn't my name, but it was something for us to chuckle
over, years later, when he showed up during my shift at Subway

to ask for my phone number. He was the first boy
to rape me, to wear my resistance thin

as the sheet on a single mattress as I searched
the ceiling for explanation. This was what I had wanted

wasn't it, to love the boy with the wry smile asking
Can you forgive me, I know your name's not Amy.

When I Think of Him Now

I think instep, ankles,
knee joints.
I think groin and solar plexus.
Windpipe. Eyes.

Vagus Nerve

What impressed me, while watching the video, was not only that the pug peed for over four minutes, but that he walked on his front legs the entire time, his bladder capacity exceeded only by his balance & commitment to the performance, and I thought surely he'd been trained, but then I recalled my friend Delainy's dog who would not shit on level ground, but had to make his statement on a rock, a ledge, a curb, the turd had to land higher than the ground he stood on or he would not shit, and I think most of us make life interesting in the ways that suit us, so why would I expect non-human animals to be any different, and all this gets me thinking about the vagus nerve—named for the Latin root *vagrant*—which wanders from the pleasure centres of the brain to the throat & heart & lungs to the guts & reproductive organs and arrives for its final curtsey at the anus, and how there's really little wonder that butt play is so damn good, that an excellent shit is satisfying beyond mere relief, delicious enough to make nipples tighten and a chorus of goosebumps sing the length of the body, sing like the squeeze of salivary glands as one hand reaches for the strawberry and the other wipes at your chin, sing like the wreck of mascara at the arrivals gate for the airplane you've been waiting on for three and a half months, so maybe this dog had discovered that urinating while walking on his forelegs with his hindquarters arching back towards his brain was his way of vagus nerve activation, the entire glory length of it, so all hail the fluffy internet star and his pleasure, all hail the wandering eccentric animals, we happy foaming beasts, we antlered beauties in our mud.

Renovation Suggestions for the Childhood Home

A blowtorch to the kitchen table, the plastic

surface melted
        into a slow wide smile.

        Pastel raindrops drawn over the ghastly
                linoleum, all that   orange
and brown retired.

    Patio stones torn
from the crabapple's roots.

        Small altars in the living room
                with offerings
          for the three dead gerbils, two cats.

Each whispered unhappiness   scraped
        from closet walls.

     A decade of journals buried

     in the backyard.

7,000 candles blazing
    in the basement,

        glitter shaken   over cobwebs, corners
   quivering.

   Skylights hacked
     into the bedroom ceilings,
mosquito netting hung

       over the beds.

Snowdrifts in winter. Spectacular

                            moulds in the carpets by early May.

             Grasshoppers creeping in by August,
                   clicking

from the light   fixtures.

Flare Up

Plainsong, the bones'
argument. Housed
in a listless machine.

Quick translation: you were better, now you're not.

But just past the binary of broken & cured
an open envelope wide as insomnia
holds your best lines.

You're center stage, dressed
in what the weather has left you
chanting *beginner, beginner, always*
beginner

The Taxidermist

In the last year of my childhood
mama turns into a deer.

>We see it coming, a tail
>flicking, a white warning flash just above her jeans, the fits

>>of whole-body trembling.

The changes come and go. Mostly she passes as human.

Some days she shuffles
as if on hooves hidden inside shoes.

>I roll my eyes, hiss *Get it together*
>when I catch her licking road salt.

Mama becomes more
>unpredictable,

>>ears lengthening and twitching.

She stomps a foot at traffic noises, stares mutely

'til I lead her home.

Father makes rough jokes about rutting season.

Late one night I hear *GodDAMNit Sheila!*
from their bedroom—

>she must have sprouted fur
>in an inconvenient place.

The night Father backhands
my brother for the way
        he handles a fork,

mama makes a strange bleating sound

then falls
        silent, looks me in the eyes one last time.

                I want to spit at her elongating face.

Reddish-brown fur ripples over skin, her hands
        harden into perfect black hooves.

She drops to all fours, leaps

                        through the kitchen window,

        bounds across the yard and over the fence.

We sit stunned
                in a hail of broken glass, blood
        beading from forearms and faces.

Shortly after, Father stops speaking,
spends most nights alone working in the basement.

        One day I come home
        to find a doe's head stuffed

                and mounted on the wall over my bed.

Love Letter to the Body

all words transcribed from the Hawthorn Farms seed catalogue

You sacred sail.
You roadside
    cascade. You greening
gargle. You naked
    magnesium glow.
You wintersown
storehouse. You mountain,
    you mouse.
You necessary
    cosmonaut.
        You scissored

                hawk, wing-snapping
                in the wind—

                        Each night is a vitamin
                        the size of the sky
                        & you,
                        necessary mountain,
                        hawk-naked & greening,

                        you get to taste
                        all you want.

General Anxiety

How it curls into the shadow
behind your ear, the small bowl

of your navel, the dip above your left
clavicle. How it fills

with its keening, burrowing in like a tick.
This always happens. You've tried

lit matches, digging nails.
It resists, knows your crevices better

than you do. Hangs on with claws, grows
extra limbs, hisses, expands as you contract.

How you'd carve it out at the cost
of pieces of your flesh, blood soaking your hair.

      And yet there was that day, that

                week,

                    when it slid

                        free.

             Headed off

         on eager feet to follow

            scent trails

in long grass; happy, for the moment,
and so were you.

Five Weeks Before I Left That House

The first and only time my father apologized
to me, he entered my room without knocking,
sat on my bed—didn't ask—dropped his *Sorry* onto the floor
like something heavy no one could be bothered to bury.

It seared a hole through the carpet, sent up a twist of smoke
and the stink of scorched nylon.

I remember looking up, my wooden eyes
tracking his face finding nowhere to land.
His mouth: nineteen years of drought,
coughing up dead fish for my lap.

His mother had mostly cured him of a bad stutter as a child
sitting by his bed at night, saying to his sleep, *You speak well.*
You speak so, so well. I like to think that she spoke it as a prayer.
That there were times when he knew he was loved.

I wonder now if he'd rehearsed beforehand,
if he was trying to say *I l-love you*
before I was gone.

HOW ARE YOU TODAY

One doesn't see it coming.
Just a few *imfines*—
easy, bland,
common as mud.

How quickly they multiply,
click into place,
sleek rows of tight teeth
piling higher than sound
until no one knows
if behind the wall
lies a thin blue wail:

waitnoactuallyiveneverbeenfine

In Defense of the Pigeon

What if I told you that pigeons recognize human faces, if you're mean to a pigeon it doesn't forget? What if I told you that pigeons mate for life and *both* parents feed milk to their babies? What if I told you that feeding chickens pigeon milk makes them grow 38% faster? Or that the pigeon never asked to be milked to grow chicken?

What if I told you that Noah's Dove was probably a homing pigeon, that it's a mystery how they find their way back? Or that the pigeon has never asked to be taken from its home? Did I mention that Paul Reuter used pigeons to run his first news agency, flying updates on the stock exchange between Berlin and Paris? Because pigeons were faster than trains? (Pigeons! Faster than trains!) Or that right now, the pigeons at the Royal Exchange buildings in London are perching, preening and shitting on Paul Reuter's statue?

Have we talked about how King George the First declared all pigeon shit to be property of the crown, because it was used to make a crucial ingredient in gunpowder? Or about how passenger pigeons once flew in flocks so dense and wide that they blocked out a mile of sky for three days at a time? There were billions—and they almost all got shot. The last passenger pigeon spent her life in a cage and died the loneliest death in the history of the world in 1914. If a rat was born with wings, wouldn't we call it a miracle?

Someone once told me about a little-known British wartime experiment in which pigeons were bred to travel great distances underwater. They were trained to swim suicide missions to sabotage German U-boats.

What if I told you that noise they make is *not* cooing, but pigeon laughter at our attempts to curb their populations by putting birth control into their feed? Have you ever noticed that people who hate pigeons also hate rats, cockroaches, and other creatures that are going to outlive them?

Have you seen that man who sits for hours on a bench by the parking lot. Do you think he's meditating. Or drunk. Does he like how on a grey day pigeons' feathers are the prettiest colours around. Does he wonder why pigeons peck at invisible things. How pigeons stick heads under wings and sleep through rush hour. How pigeons perch on one foot forever because the other one's missing.

Pigeons are like that. They carry on.

Little Sister

My sister and I hatch from the same egg,
sleep in a nest in the backyard maple,
climb down once a day to trick food from strangers,
grow feathers instead of pubic hair. No, sorry.
We're a normal family. My sister and I share
the toilet, tiny bums pressed together on the seat to pee.
Everyone asks if we're twins and we lie proudly: *Yes.*
We scramble onto the school roof, collect lost tennis balls
and sell them back to the boys. We wear spaghetti straps.
Freckle across the shoulders. Race our bikes downtown
to dive off the docks at the harbourfront
—no, that was someone else. We read books
in acceptable dresses. Dad locks us up anyway. The only
light a crack between the door and the floor
at the top of the basement stairs. She and I fight
over mouldy bread, the one thin blanket.
We tell each other the best lies at night
when one of us can't sleep: *Mom and Dad love
each other. Mom's divorcing Dad and we'll get to live with her.*
My sister smokes weed in the mall parking lot during gym class
and Mr. Mathison calls our parents. I don't let Dad hit
her, run screaming at his face with a butterknife.
We steal the car after I get my learner's permit,
drive it across the frozen lake to Wolfe Island
on Christmas Eve, lie on our backs at the edge
of the ice watching the stars. We never get caught.
We're invincible. Dad calls me a witch, sets fire
to my hair, and compliments my sister's blonde braid.
I've worn a wig of feathers ever since. Just kidding.
It's not how it sounds. Before I leave for college,
my sister and I pledge never to suck in our stomachs
for a guy. Later, amend it *for anyone.*

When the pills don't work she calls me in the night.
Tell me a really good lie, will you? She's the first
to say, *Your girlfriend controls you just like Dad controls Mom.*
Doesn't judge me for it. When her black kitten goes missing
I fly out to Montréal to walk the parks with her calling his name.
I'm sure that happened. I remember the frozen little corpse.
When I do my first poetry tour she brings her friends,
coworkers, three roommates and two—no—three dozen roses.
Sits beaming in the front row at three different shows.
Isn't jealous. When Dad arrives at the Ottawa show
she helps my girlfriend kick him out. *This isn't for you.*
Get the fuck out of here. When her baby comes three months early
I spend the night on a blue plastic chair in ICU.
My tiny niece: my sun and my moon. I promise
to give her Great-Great Aunt Emma's necklace
when she's older. We plan how to take care of Mom
when Dad finally dies. Sorry, I've misled you: I am
an only child. I hatched alone, raised myself
and don't miss anything.

THE SUMMER I WAS SIXTEEN

I wear a hot pink LGBT Pride t-shirt
from the Queen's University Womyn's
Center. There's a photo of me
in the paper between Steph Hockerty
and Molly Laird, trying to appear
as if it's not my first parade.
I'm not cool enough to be queer. It takes
me three years to come out.
Molly lines her eyes and her lips with blue
eyeliner, leans in to the mirror
on the inside of her locker. I cry
too often for makeup. Steph rolls
her t-shirt to her shoulders to expose
the black triangle tattoo on her bicep.
I can't even roll my own joints.
They know the names of the clerks
with interesting haircuts
at the independent bookstore.
They tongue-kiss girls
on school nights and stroll in late
to first period, rolling their eyes
at how tired they are, how satisfied.
I understand I'm lacking
some basic sophistication. My laugh's
too eager. I have a bland face.
The boyfriend is an appendage
I haven't figured out how to amputate.
I know I don't want to die without
becoming someone I could fall in love with.
I try to place myself near the queers
without seeming desperate, drink
my coffee black in downtown cafés

reading Chrystos, Jeannette Winterson,
Pat Califia. If I study the gay girls,
maybe I could become careless,
loose-limbed and unapologetic.
If I were invited to their parties,
it could rub off on me. Like glitter
so cool it never caught the light.

The Divorce Party

When the holes in the boat
you shared become bigger
than your bravest bucket,
and you stop bailing

once you've swum to opposite
shores, running the risk of the loneliest
pneumonia, there will be
the Divorce Party:

an ending celebration
with a gift registry.

You are sleeping alone now,
but here is a toaster.

Here we witness
your anger, your panic, the spasms
of grief, your secret relief,
reminding you that even with blue
lips and numb limbs you are better
off now than you were, that this ending
does not happen in isolation.
We will not accept *fine* as an answer
from you for the next year.

The brave face has no place
at the Divorce Party
as you shiver in a towel
with mascara on your cheeks
gripping a mug of tea,
as you stagger backwards

along the aisle and crumple
partway through, as we cut
the cake, smash the plate,
and raise a toast to the new beginnings
only permitted by a death.
We're heading off the possibility
of an ill-advised reconciliation.
After tonight there'll be no resurrection—
and no mention of how long you two
dragged it out. We name this
completion, never failure,
thank you for loving so
fiercely, so unwisely.

While contemplating the impossible
beast of finality, what is hardest
for you to ask for?
Are you eating? Are your hip
and collarbones protruding
the way they do when you want
to disappear?

At the Divorce Feast we spill
your favourite foods down our fronts
while making inappropriate jokes
and swinging between laughing,
weeping and cussing. This is for us, too.
We thought you'd be together
forever. And now we incur
grease stains on our finery
finding dignity in solidarity—

here is the collection to cover damage
deposit at your new flat,

here is the list of numbers to call
when you cannot sleep,
here are blessings of equal
velocity to catastrophe,
here is how you grow large enough
for your own life.

My Grandma's Poetry

A response to the branding of performance poetry as "Not Your Grandma's Poetry."

My grandma's poetry lived through eight decades,
buried one son, and painfully came to accept
that her other son was broken,
to the point of being cruel to children,
and she loved him anyways.

My grandma's poetry is teaching me
about forgiveness.

My grandma's poetry married a violent alcoholic
then hid the marriage because back then,
only single women worked outside the home,
and they needed the money.

My grandma's poetry knows the combined bite
of poverty and misogyny.

My grandma's poetry calls
her nineteen-year-old queer granddaughter
to say *I love you, the whole you,*
and I am so happy you know yourself.

My grandma's poetry wants to know
what you hate about the elderly?

My grandma's poetry talks to ghosts,
honours compost, attends births in the dark.
It spins, weaves, and mends,
will probably be appropriated at some point,
is quietly appalled by rooms of storytellers
who'd dismiss old women as conservative

or boring, and perceives the links between
male-dominated slam scenes
and rape culture.

My grandma's poetry is reclaiming *crone,*
hag, witch and old wives' tales,
is medicine, lineage and anchor.

My grandma's poetry lives in the deepest
of listening, reminds us of our mortality,
sits next to me while I write,
nods at my laugh lines and tells me

Darling, when you are a grandma,
you'll be one hell of a poet.

Touch

Touch the steamed glass, the water heater secretly switched almost to scalding. Bathroom door locked—Mom says *You could drown in there and we wouldn't know*—but you are slick and clever in bright foam, shaving cream, pink razor a curious flamingo in your hand touching your skin new.

The bathroom where you discover your blood, first blessing of brown on your underwear and say a secret *thank god.*

Touch the skim of your skin on sheets, no lock on the bedroom door but three more years until you leave and never come back.

But you were alive. Don't say you were half-dead, when you weren't.

Touch the MacDougall's fence on the way to visit Sarah, just for the swing up and over, the chain-link metal smell on your palms. Touch the dry paper curl of that first joint with Katie on the breakwater. You think it hasn't hit you, then float from rock to jagged rock, leap towards the middle of the lake, your head a laughing ship. You could make it rain with a wish. You make love to that lake, swim in it alone each summer despite warnings of pollution, wringing out your underwear on the dock afterwards.

Touch how hard you try to do what you want with that body.

Numb knuckles to turquoise linoleum, the cabinet shelf of codeine, Tylenol 1, Tylenol 2, far too bitter to chew. The bathroom where the white-hot pain in your spine first hurls you against the counter, gaping at yourself in the mirror unable to breathe. Only eleven and struggling to bend, to walk. They say you were such a sensitive child.

But also the smell of your own skin just below the elbow when it is touched by sun and wind. Your sister smells herself there too; you compare sweat and know each other. Sun burning your backs, slow-melting the tar on the roof where you sit overlooking Princess St. Agreeing it is some tired bullshit girls don't climb to roofs more often. Touch the minutes you had a sister before your father took that away too.

Touch Megan Channing's lower lip, slipping into your boyfriend's bathroom to let her press you against the sink, as if you don't know what she wants from your mouth.

Touch tiny hammers raining across mother's dulcimer, which mean she is happy and father is out or not angry. Touch when you could hope for an end to his anger.

Touch the cat rumbling on your chest, licking your chin, nipping hard at your lower lip then settling in the doorway to guard your sleep.

You were alive. The thick dark night. The scent lake water makes on your skin.

IV

WINDBREAK

all words transcribed from the Hawthorn Farms seed catalogue

When deadheaded stars fall
from a plastic sky

& the heart is a pinched moth
too slow to travel with wild deer,

the naked wound is a bridge.
Is a raw gift to the weather. Once joy

was evergreen. An electric egg.
A golden holy flock. Love,

that bright-tongued workhorse:
magic, multibranching.

Disappointed earthwalker, here
is a windbreak. Here a licorice

light still hangs warm in the belly
& somewhere the long throat of time

keeps summer enough for you.

Her Estranged Family Finds the Poems Online

They console each other.

Sick.

Unbalanced.

Delusional.

Turn pictures of her to face the wall. Later, yank
them out of the family album.

They get creative with history.

She was always the crazy one.

Write emails, search out her workplace,
send letters about libel.

Your mother

will never forgive you.

Father cancels the wifi, but
the unblinking eye of the internet
hovers
over their beds at night, casts blue light over their dreaming.

They don't understand they're not the audience,
that the unwritten poem burns
like stomach acid on back teeth.
That a girl's mouth is hammer,
muscle made to spit things out.

WISE & GOOD
after Patricia Smith

Daring the world
to harm us, we undo
buckles, touch wood, rattle
fire escapes. We quit searching
for decent lighting to read by,
for an honest name, & thank
our eyes for working at all.
It is hard to focus beyond the damage.
I never tried for shatterproof. This
is my best tarnish. This
will not be new again. But
my body is wise & good
& I am mostly more
than ghost.

HARD RIME

The air here, so dry
the nosebleed scabs
on every inhale. A man
in Boston sells snow,
sending it away
in Styrofoam coolers.

> Last week frozen fog clung
> to trees & cars & houses.
> A billion tiny ghost teeth
> on the windward side
> of everything: hard rime.

I caught a ride to work today;
forty below with windchill, *Metro
Morning* said. You could hear the
wince in the newscaster's voice.
The new ergonomic shovel hurts us
less, & sometimes the neighbours
blow out the driveway.

> Steam forms crystals on the window
> over the sink, they spiderweb out
> & melt back depending on
> how long we leave the dishes,
> whether the water heater
> gives us hot or tepid.

> Sun rises over the garlic bed,
> splashes tangerine
> on the south facing wall
> a moment earlier each day.

It still takes twenty-five minutes
to trudge down the hill to the clinic.
I miss my bike. Two of our plants
have died this month
& won't compost until spring.

The river starts & stops, talks then falls
quiet, fills with ice needle-like clusters
& there's a name for that too.
Frazil ice. From the bridge,
the Speed River seems like slush,
but climb down to the riverbank
& *A-ha, Frazil,*

I announce to the ducks. They huddle
together on the shore, eighteen green
& brown & blue, feet tucked
under feathers, not waiting

for anything.

FACTS ABOUT SUNFLOWERS
after Mindy Nettifee

The tallest sunflower on record reached twenty-eight feet in Germany in August 2013. It grew upright inside protective aluminum scaffolding. The previous winner was a 26-footer climbing up the side of a two-story house in Wigan, UK. The lesson here is that sunflowers prefer aluminum to brick.

Raccoons decapitate sunflower seedlings and leave them to rot in the dark. Raccoons do a lot of strange destructive things for no apparent reason. But they could say the same about us.

The Fibonacci sequence was discovered in India but is named after a European. In a Fibonacci sequence each subsequent number is the sum of the previous two. Fibonacci sequences appear in the arrangement of leaves on a stem, the uncurling of a fern, and the seed spirals in every sunflower's face.

Sunflowers are famous mathematicians.

Last summer when my amygdala locked herself inside with the sharpest knives and smashed every dish while my hippocampus and higher cortex slumped in a corner staring at the wall, the only thing that stopped the screaming was the toothy yellow throng in front of the house.

Sunflowers stand guard.

The chickadees at Starkey Hill will pluck sunflower seeds from your upturned palm, will flash down from their branches to astonish your skin with the whisk of tiny wings, the hollow-boned weight of their trust, how they keep kissing your fingers with their feet, even though you are just some girl with seeds cupped in her palm.

IT HAS BEEN FOUR DAYS SINCE YOU READ ABOUT THE MONARCHS

You too, are doomed. You've known
this for years but the end of this winged thing has thrust
past every defense and you've been mourning for days;
destruction of forest means the monarch hasn't
much to cling to. The inside of your mind's a grey sky,
your heart dry and still, some small part
of you whispering *so this is despair.*

It's the compost that gets you off the couch,
the potato peels liquefying in the kitchen's warmest
corner. You drag the dripping tub outside to dump
it over the brimming compost bin. You open up the bottom
to scent the soil at the base, fresh earth that was kitchen
scrap two months ago.

The smell is rich enough to make you weep as you pull forth
a fistful, to cry harder as you fill a cracked bucket, and to sob
as you spread a moist black layer over next year's garlic bed.
And as you fork it in, feeding life to life, you land on the other
side of despair which is where everything matters,
where tiny creatures tougher than you continue,
which is to say here is something to cling to,
and you bury both hands up to the wrists.

PERIGEE

All we knew was the moon brightened
that summer, dimmed the other lights in the sky.
When it started to seem unusually huge
some dismissed this as mass hallucination,
pointed to the etymology of the word lunacy.

Menstrual cycles were disrupted.
Datura bloomed longer and more potent.
Amateur astronomers picked out details
of the tiniest craters and maria
through toy binoculars.

As high tide soaked the first & second floors
of beachfront apartment buildings
while low tide left wider stretches of ocean floor
flinching like a dry eye, one theory
suggested that an asteroid
had knocked the moon off course.

For weeks the moon approached, slow
and terrifying. Physicists scrambled to predict
how long until tsunamis swallowed coastal cities,
until the moon's new gravitational muscle
heaved the earth's tectonic plates like a drunk
with a losing hand flipping a card table.

Everyone who was able spilled outside at moonrise,
dragged chairs to front lawns and sidewalks,
livestreamed the update to the other side of the planet.
Neighbours got beyond small talk. End of the World
parties took over our block every weekend.
People quit diets & bad jobs,

drove recklessly, said *I love you.*

The moon loomed larger
and glowed with its own yellow light
all month, yolked-open.

Scientists repeated phrases
like *inert ball of basalts and silicates*
and *cold dead mass.* No one
listened. Armed militia
climbed a mountain, took aim.
Coyotes and wolves howled,
audible in the suburbs.
Rumours circulated of an escape
plan to Mars. No one will forget
that night in August it sped up,
the collective gasp as the moon
swelled rapidly, zooming closer—

for one last good look?
to say *here's what you'll be missing?*

Even cicadas held still in the hush. Shadows
sharpened, snapped into place in the beckoning light
as the moon spun 180 degrees, showing us the other side
for the first and last time, paused—

and exited our slowdance.
Broke the ancient agreement of orbit
and swung free, leaving us alone
in an empty aching dark.

GRIEF

A gorilla so large
it can brush knuckles
against each wall
of this room
without moving
from the bed
where it straddles
your chest.

Lock eyes with it
long enough
and maybe it lets you
free an arm, crack open
a window.

Half a Heart is Like Half a Highway
after Karen Finneyfrock

Half a heart is like half a highway, stumbling
out of the car away from strained exchanges
that suck the air out of a small space but lack
the heat of a real argument. Half a highway leaves
you stranded at the side of the road, dress hem
darkening with ditchwater apologies. You could
stay long enough to feed your heart fat in this ditch.
Fill your pockets with queen anne's lace and chicory.
It will rain soon, a mumbling drizzle that struggles
to form vowels. Half a sentence, half a highway.
She stares ahead, waits in the car.

You might wonder why I wandered so deep

without a compass, without the skills
to use a compass once I had gotten lost.

I took only my grouchy self into the forest to ask
the spruce saplings and fireweed for the grace to forgive

my girlfriend for the things she'd done the previous winter—
grouchy meaning, in this case, pissed off and heartsore.

You might wonder how I went from murmuring
to the forest spirits to urgent open-throated bargaining

with god, to promising some deity
that if I got out of these woods alive I'd drop

the grudge against my girlfriend *and* her other lover.
You might wonder if the lateness

of the hour had something to do with it,
if the trickles of tiny streams, the quaking aspen,

the cheeky riot of wildflower and fern
start to lose their charm after three or four hours

of desperate circling, of where the hell
was that goddamn path, the sharp scent of fear

in my sweat, soaked from the knees down, calves
and thighs studded with devil's club thorns, the kind

you're digging out of your flesh for weeks
afterwards —if you've planted trees in BC or Alberta

you know what I mean—and let's remember
that I didn't know if I had weeks afterward,

given how skinny I am and how cold the nights
are that late in the season, my main thought

by the sixth hour *just keep moving and stay
warm* as I blundered into a hornet's nest and ran

from the indignant swarm while the sunset
painted the sky every ominous shade of red

and coyotes howled, my own throat past hoarse
from hollering for someone, anyone to help me.

Two forest officers took the back roads
to my lookout and, having no idea where I'd gone,

leaned on the truck horn until I followed that blessed
sound out of the dark toward the lit window of my cabin.

Did I keep my end of the deal?
After my girlfriend drove five hours the next day

just to give me a back-rub and fry me a steak,
was I able to forgive her?

When I think now of our breakup, years later,
all I remember is the baby bird that had fallen from the nest

to sprawl, pink and pathetic on the neighbour's driveway,
how I grabbed the shovel from where it leaned against

warm brick to sever the head from the body—
it took two tries—then rushed off, promising a decent

burial when I returned. How weakly it thrashed
when I lifted it hours later, how I had to drop it again

to smash the skull flat with the shovel. I think
of the mess that a partial decapitation makes,

when good intentions are the opposite of mercy, I think
of wracking sobs, *I'm so sorry, I didn't mean to do that*

as I buried it alone on my knees in the dark in the backyard,
wishing it could have been a briefer dying.

You might wonder why I'm circling back
to any of this, why I still can't pry it out of my flesh

having forgiven things worse than that winter, or why
I thought god would decide to save someone from hypothermia

based on whether she forgave
her girlfriend. Why this seemed the best

I could offer, worth my life in that moment,
the one thing that could get me back home.

Thank You

To Rachel McKibbens for editing an early version of this manuscript. To Adèle Barclay for editing the final version. To Anna Swanson, David James Hudson, Lisa Rohleder, Shira Erlichman, Jeanann Verlee, Megan Falley, gillian harding-russell & Wolfgang Chrapko for helping to shape and polish some or many of these poems. To David James Hudson & Helen Hudson for helping me think through issues around land acknowledgements. To Vancouver Poetry Slam & Guelph Spoken Word. To Hawthorn Farm for producing a seed catalogue containing such wonderful words. To the team at Caitlin Press for working patiently and diligently with me on the creation of this book. To Anna Swanson for holding my hand through every step of this process.

CREDITS

Thank you to the editors of the publications which gave homes to the following poems

"Welcome to the Museum of Art-Based Apology" and "Five Weeks Before I Left That House" in *Apeiron Review*

"Facts About Sunflowers" in *Arc Poetry Magazine*

"The Taxidermist" in *CV2*

"Hex" and "Grief" in *Drunk in a Midnight Choir*

"Winter's Cold Girls" in *Grain Magazine*

"TAMPAX LOVES YOU, GIRL" in *GUSH: Menstrual Manifestos for Our Times* (Frontenac House, 2018)

"Galaxy" and "Wise & Good"in *Hematopoiesis*

"The Word for Secrets" in *Plenitude Magazine*

"Hard Rime" in *PRISM International*

"Facts About Dead Trees" and "Reasons for Ambivalence about Growing My Hair Out" in *Poetry Is Dead*

"Vagus Nerve" in *Rattle*

"You might wonder why I wandered so deep," "Burnpile" and "Renovation Suggestions for the Childhood Home" in *Thalia Magazine*

"When I Think of Him Now," "Windbreak" and "To the Anti-Abortion Organization That Raised $91,000 to Build an Abortion-and-Miscarriage Grieving Garden Complete with a Statue of Jesus Holding a Dead Baby" in *The Anti-Langorous Project*

"Aftermath" in *The Golden Key*

"Her Estranged Family Finds the Poems Online" in *Winter Tangerine Review*

About the Author

Vanessa Tignanelli photo

Lisa Baird is a poet, a community acupuncturist and a queer white settler living on the territories of the Attawandaron/Chonnonton people, and of the Mississaugas of the Credit Anishnaabek people. (Also known as Guelph, ON. Also known more broadly as Canada. Also known as an ongoing project of genocide and erasure, some of which is accomplished through word craft, which seems worth mentioning in a book of poetry.) Her poetry has appeared in various literary journals and she is a contributor to the Lambda Literary Award–winning anthology *The Remedy: Queer and Trans Voices on Health and Healthcare* (Arsenal Pulp Press, 2016) and to *GUSH: Menstrual Manifestos for Our Times* (Frontenac House, 2018).

www.lisabaird.ca